Through a *Faery Stone*

The Secret World of Faerie

Paintings by Ed Hicks

Words by Dee Stotts

Through a Faery Stone

The Secret World of Faerie

Published by
AAPPL Artists' and Photographers' Press Ltd.
Church Farm House, Wisley, Surrey GU23 6QL
info@aappl.com   www.aappl.com

Sales and Distribution
UK and Export: Turnaround Publisher Services Ltd
orders@turnaround-uk.com
USA and Canada: Sterling Publishing Inc sales@sterlingpub.com
Australia & New Zealand: Peribo Pty Ltd michael.coffey@peribo.com.au
South Africa: trinity Books trinity@iafrica.com

A catalogue record for this book is available from the British Library.

ISBN trade edition   1904332722   9781904332725
ISBN boxed edition   1904332773   9781904332770

Design (contents and cover): Stefan Nekuda office@nekuda.at

Printed in China by: Imago Publishing
info@imago.co.uk

Through a
Faery Stone

The Secret World of Faerie

Paintings by Ed Hicks
Words by Dee Stotts

what faeries are really about

By John Grant

Many years ago, when the world was a fresher place than it is today, an old woman and a young one were bringing home baskets of mushrooms for the family pot. The day was still not properly awake, and their breath made clouds as they clambered down the steep side of a small gorsy hill. Every so often the young woman would pause and reach out an arm for her grandmother to grab hold of, even though her grandmother didn't need the support.

At the foot of the slope was a lake - little more than a pond, really. In the tentative warmth of the new day's sun, mist was rising from the still surface.

When the two women came to the water's edge, the grandmother told her young companion to stop there a while, claiming she needed to catch her breath back. The young woman was impatient to be home, but she hid this. Standing side by side, their baskets on their arms in front of them, the two looked out at the low-lying whiteness of the mist.

"What can you see there, child?" said the grandmother, pointing.

The girl shrugged. "Just the warmth of the sunlight making steam come up from the water. I wish a bit of that warmth would get through to me. I'm chilled to the bone. I don't think I'll ever heat up. You must be even colder than I am, Grandma. Your bones are closer to the skin than mine."

"Can't you see them dancing?"

The young woman obediently stared, but all she could see was mist. Something - it must be a light wind, although she couldn't feel any breeze on her hands or face - was making the topmost layers of the mist move in slow, graceful spirals as they rose and listlessly vanished into the air.

"I can see them dancing," she said, humouring her grandmother. She was a well brought-up young woman and knew to show respect for her elders, even when they were especially tiresome.

The mist continued to rise, continued to thin into the air. The sun didn't seem to be growing any brighter, though. Or warmer. Even the birds weren't singing. The young woman shivered.

"We'd best be getting on home now, Grandma."

"No. Wait a moment longer, girl. Keep watching until you see them."

"I told you, I already can -"

"You told me a lie. I'd have done the same if I'd been you, sent out before daybreak with a cantankerous old -"

The girl giggled, although not with much conviction. "You aren't cantankerous, Grandma."

"Maybe not always, but I'm certainly old. So bear with me a few minutes more, child, until you can see the Finefolk dance."

The young woman breathed very deeply, and she waited, and watched, and after more than a few minutes passed she still couldn't see anyone dancing, but she did see the mist disappear from the face of the pond entirely.

"They were there," said the old woman at last, turning to walk along the side of the water. If she'd been on her own she might just have waded through the pond, which wasn't deep, but that wasn't the kind of thing a respectable woman did when her grandchild was there. "I could see them as clear as day. They were taking their Queen to welcome the dawn, and they were dancing as they went."

She's not going to be with us much longer, thought the young woman sadly, following behind her, hanging back so as not to collide with her. Poor old dear. If you listen carefully you can hear her arthritis creak.

That was when, out of the very corner of her eye, she saw the flicker of a tiny wing.

When she turned to look, it was gone.

A very long time later, she stood by the side of that same pond and watched as her own granddaughters, two of them, pretended to see the faeries when they couldn't.

But she could.

Dark Faery

Dark Innocence

Darkness lures you
With eyes of promise
Soft pouty lips
Blood-red wings of velvet
Pure silken hair
Trails over lace-covered bosoms
You see a welcome here
A hint of softness
Akin to the petal of a rose
And you wonder
What the night holds
Will you find your heart
Or lose your soul
In its pursuit
You step toward her
And through the wooden door
To the world beyond
The wall of stone
Light behind you flickers
And extinguishes
There is no return

I love you, pretty Hummingbird

Hi!

Reflection

REFLECTION

Will he think me beautiful today
Water mirror tell your secrets
Is the flower too much
Release from your depths what you know
His whispered words you have heard
I know this to be true

Will he think me beautiful today
Water mirror tell your secrets
Does my bosom he long to touch
Release from your depths what you know
My body craves his caress
You know this to be true

Will he think me beautiful today
Water mirror tell your secrets
Will his hand trace my skin as does the breeze
Release from your depths what you know
Do together we belong forever
I so long this to be true

Will he think me beautiful today
Water mirror tell your secrets

Little Faery in the Garden

Queen of the May

BOG FAERY

Black clouds scud across a gray-green sky
Like age spots on an enormous bosom pressing down
Damp Spanish moss sways slightly in a swirl of humid air
Such a dark, dismal place is this sweltering bog
Charcoal trees thrust skyward out of the mire
Dank mist rolls across the water's surface, rises like smoke
Just when it appears there is nothing pretty here
Upon a stone, a faery curls her legs beneath her
Toes of one foot trail in the tepid water
Like a lover, the liquid laps her skin
Gossamer wings catch and cast pink light about
Soft mouth and doey eyes emit such tenderness
Beg without words for you to readjust your mind
Quiet can be heard, but more now that you can see
Your own pink light flickers within your soul
Such is the way to see beauty in its imperfection
A look is exchanged between you two
You shiver despite the balmy air and she smiles

Bog Faery

Rodina

Berries

DAISY FAERY

Basking in afternoon temperatures just so
Daisy Faery whispers age-old wisdom
No matter what life sends to your door
You must always pause to turn face skyward
Heaven awaits to bestow blessed peace
In stillness will it find and cascade over you
Take a lesson from a sunny-faced flower
Stretch your neck and tilt your head
Breathe deep and soft—savor every one
Commune with the inner self you are
Explore that place you may have forgotten
When at last you open your eyes
Trouble will be smaller than before
If it is not, at least you will have found the sun
And in it, the promise you know it holds

Daisy Faery

Night Faery

NIGHT FAERY

Night has come in its delicious glory
Midnight blue chases ebony across the sky
Sensual sounds emanate though the pines
Luscious lips purse in anticipation of what next comes
Talon-tipped fingers slide around in corn silk hair
Leathery wings unwrap a delectable torso
Milky skin - such sweet contrast to the dark
An owl hoots, a wolf howls, emerald eyes close
A sigh escapes, breathy and bold
Ancient pewter loops suspend a scarlet pendant
The valley of her bosom cradles the brilliant crystal
She stands, inhales the starless night
Takes air to share her charms, pleasure on her mind

Coronation of the Faery Queen

Bat Faery

WHEN TEARS FALL

Heartache races across the plain
Shades of darkness haunt
Pain permeates tender flesh
Emptiness consumes
In the harshness of betrayal
Bended knee
A prayer to Mother Earth
Promise in a breath of wind
And the sweetness of Father Time
Allow room to be melancholy

Melancholy

Seasons change

DEAR FRIEND

My dear friend
Of dusty wing
Here comes the nonsense
Of haphazardly connected
Ice crystals
And frigid wind
Gone will be the lovely green
You and I love to fly
The realm will be consumed
With an encompassing white
Months will pass
Before it's May
And again the flowers unfurl
I will miss you though the silence
My dear friend
Of dusty wing

Fascination

Indian Faery

Faery with Koi

Barn Faeries

BARN MOMENT

Rough-hewn wood
A refuge of hay
Fragrant aroma
Simple respite
Ordinary place
Effortless love
Playful magic
Grace added
Least expected
Quiet place
Gentle commune
Contentment

Shelter

Cavorting with the Chipmunks

NATURE SPIRIT

Clarity
Purity
Unclothed, unchained
Spiritual
Sensual
Earth connected
Simplicity
Transparency
To the sky allied
Wholesomeness
Intelligence
Untouched caress
Natural
Beautiful
Faery ideal

Nature Spirit

Faery Mother and Child

Girl talk

Admiration

NOT JUST A MORTAL DREAMS

A faery grows herself to the length of the bathing girl
Who dreams of mushroom rings and realms unknown
Oblivious to the reality that is just beside her
Relishing her new larger size
The faery wonders about life without wings
How must it feel to be forever clothed
And never to upon a toadstool dance
To have to always walk upon the ground
Tickly grass under the bottoms of your feet
"It is you who has the better dream"
She whispers softly to the mortal girl
The human turns beneath the falls
Just as the faery flits away

Linnea and a Ladybug

Sabrina

Hide and Seek

seashore faery

In a peachy shell beside the sea
A tiny beauty prepares for slumber
Dusk wraps the shore in twilight blue
And pulls a yawn from deep within
Waves hum gently in ebbing tide
Silence becomes a peaceful backdrop
As feathers call forth relaxation
Salty air comforts and caresses
In this time when night cloaks the sky

Sleeping on the beach

Playing with Barkley

Irish Faery

WARRIOR PRINCESS

A fae of fierce beauty and strength
Defends her territory relentlessly
Leather and bone shield her breast
Adorn her wrists, her ankles and neck
She rides a bobcat on perimeter patrol
Diligent and prepared for anything, anyone
To cross her path, unsuspecting or not
Fury unleashed—perhaps they would survive
Or blessed mercy—to become the fallen
So 'tis best not to cross the boundary
Take a different path, mere mortal
Fly another route above the trees, dear fae
Pray don't engage on this day or another
Back straight, shoulders proud
Eyes always scanning, never does she stop
A fae of fierce beauty and strength
Defends her territory relentlessly

Warrior Princess

Resting place

RESTING PLACE

Her body supported by mushroom foam
A faery peruses the wood
Ruffle-y transport upon her back
Birds twitter in the trees
Peace plays across her face
Calm has a home here
In this cool, quiet place
Boughs rustle overhead
Butterflies flitter by
She twitches antennae
Pleasure skitters down her spine
She hurries not, but rests a while

Faery sunbathing on a rock

A Faery in my hand

Michele with her Wolf

OLD FRIENDS

A sky of fire stretches taut between mountain stone
But the majesty is in the eyes of accompanied lone wolf
Sitting regal upon his coat, a faery sinks her hand within
It is not often she chooses such transportation over flight
Yellow orbs glow from their depths with pride of this knowledge
A kindred bond links these two - something that began long ago
Upon a chance meeting, when a child-faery and a cub collided
Nose to nose in a fragrant field one gray and foggy morning
They stared at each other in shock and surprise - she giggled
He snuffled - his breath sent her tumbling through the air
Shrill laughter pierced the quiet - then a playful growl
A shoulder drops and a paw twice pats the ground
Memory clouds her eyes at the familiar gesture
She smiles and whispers as he turns his head
One blessing and eons later - the gift is not forgotten

MORNING SHOWER

Bare skin meets stone
On a crystal morn

From slickened leaves
Droplets fall
Onto slender fae
With reddish hair

A cleansing comes
On a crystal morn

When air is snappy
With chill of night
Whispering against
Dampened skin

A private moment
On a crystal morn

Faery perfection
Becomes pristine
Like the water
Falling from above

Liquid refreshment
On a crystal morn

Early morning Shower

19 Fabulous flirtatious Faery of green

Mood swiny

The Faery Sonia

FAERY INSIDE

What goes on behind that frame of petals
Is there
Bountiful sunshine and flower perfume
Or does
Beauty belie withered buds and stagnant air
Such a face
Cannot be read from the outer surface
Yet how
How does one get beyond the skin
Those eyes
Avert from the invasion they can sense
Never
Will the inner world of mossy transparence
Be seen
Always will it be hidden from understanding
It is
Forever concealed, the secret faery inside

Pretty little Faery setting on a tree eating berries

Decorating for the holidays

Sleeping together

UNLIKELY FRIEND

Skin on fur
Slumber fast
Jungle friend
Safe at last
Rise and fall
Rocks me best
Strong sinew
Stands the test
Eyes are closed
Not the mind
Fleeting fast
No rewind
Careful step
Shallow breath
Shall evade
Certain death

ON A MISSION

A raven-haired faery with crimson lips
Barrels through the dark on midnight wing
Mouth drawn back in frightful grimace
Blade at her side, casts silver flashes
Eyes aglow with some hard hatred
Buried deep within her soul, it burns
A fine sweat glistens on porcelain skin
Such beautiful anger would not be squashed
It travels onward with force unparalleled
One thing is definite on this night
Blood will spill as certain as her blade is steel

Underworld Faery

Angelou

Another Awesome Day!!

BEAUTIFUL DANGER

Some faeries should be viewed from a distance
There may be no moving water to leap across
To escape the wildness they convey
Should you venture beyond your bounds
Individual becomes synonymous
With reckless abandon soul
These faeries perceive no need for finesse
Exist only to satisfy their every whim
When confronted with raw intensity
As emanates from such a being
You will crumble—all senses lost
The very thing you thought delicate and fair
Will ream your core to quivering
All known defense will become forgotten
Will trap you forever in fairyland
A hapless human slave

Some Faeries are to be watched from a distance

Protectors

Faery in the morning dew

Plant Faery

THE BUTTERCUP QUEEN

A playful day in buttercups
Peek-a-boo, a smile or two
Coyness manifest
Utter bliss personified
Michaela, Michaela
On such a delicious morning
Curls entangle pointy blades
As sunshine reflects on wings
Tiny body folded onto itself
Queen amongst bright petals
A beauty on the ground
Michaela, Michaela

Michaela in Buttercups

Faery in my Garden

Bead Faery

FAERY OF THE FIRE

At times there is need only for a flicker
And she calmly complies
Providing gentle light in hot points
For her it is effortless
Extending from her fingers in a caress
She savors these times
When the flame can be small and easy
But she positively animates
During the times she can give her all
She coaxes small blue tongues
That dance upon a white-hot bed
"Come", she beckons
And yellow-orange spires burst forth
She is jubilant
Her body carried on invisible current
Up where she can peruse
The maelstrom of licking fire
It reaches for her
As she twirls ever higher
Colors of heat nudge and shove
Try to gain her favor
At last she comes to them
And waltzes in their midst

Fire Faery

In the Dogwoods

Flower Faery

APRIL, EARTH FAIRY

This is what I do
Bring life forth from the earth
Not on my own, mind you
Mother Nature has that job
But I am here for the birth
Such miracle sets me sigh
The earth so warm and firm
Gives back what it takes
In shades of green
Empty blue skies
Caresses of bright heat
Two friends come to crawl
Newborn ivy laces around me
I am willingly captured

All manner of beings

Faery with a Daisy

The Faery Judith

A touch of Love

MIDNIGHT MAGIC

What happens when you slumber
And your mind is besieged
What reality becomes you
What magic touches your being
With a spark of light and hope
To keep at bay the darkness
So that when you awaken
Love overcomes you
And takes you to a place
Beyond your usual realm
Somewhere pixie dust falls
Fireflies light the sky
And tiny fae dance inside a circle
With you at the centre

Faery with a Butterfly

The Faery Michele

Camouflage

CAMOUFLAGE

Where do you go
When you don't want the world to see you
You hide
In plain sight
They never see you there, in front of their eyes
You show them
Colors they wish to see
Wrap them all around yourself, completely
You disappear
Yet there you are
But no one looks close enough to see you
You blend in
With the background
It's clever and foolproof, never breached
And yet
What's that
A spear of heat, pricking carefully laid armor
Prompting you
To peek out
And so you unfurl just a little to see what it is
And now
Oh, now
The real you is exposed and the hurt can come
Will you stay
Or cocoon
Is it worth the pain to ditch the camouflage
And so
Your eyes speak
And your wings wrap you tightly once more
And there you are
Gone again

Tiffany in the Gaura

Painting a Faery Portrait

The first Crocus of Spring

Faery on a rock

A need for Peace

A NEED FOR PEACE

Moonlight changes white-blond locks to molten silver
A brittle wind sends prickles along pale skin
Water murmurs faintly as it courses beneath her
She leans in to better hear its words of wisdom
A yearning to be free of turmoil evident on her face
The ache in her heart almost palpable in the night
Where she is now is the place to come for restoration
The endless rolling of the river brings peace at will
So they converse until the night fades subtly away

The Faery Lori

Dandelions

BOTTOMNESS

Gray smothers
My breath arrests
Earthen crevices
Threaten to devour
What mystery
How my hide
Crashed into
This bottomness
Elevated answers
Elude my mind
But to transcend
I spread my wings

Waiting for darkness

Imp

PRANKSTER

It was so funny when they fell on their fannies
The loosened toadstool caps all askew on the ground
Then when the berries rained down on their heads——
It was the best formal dinner of my life
They all looked at me——I couldn't hide my grin
I gave my frog a little squeeze
Getting grounded from using my glamour——
Well, that was worth it anyway
I'd do it again in a second——I would
I love to see their faces——it cracks me up inside
They glare at me and say my ears are horns
Always tell me they're on their guard
But I surprise them every single time
And guess what
I got my glamour back today

Faery energy

If you know what's good for you you'll leave me alone today!

Two Faeries Bathing

GLIMPSE THROUGH A STONE

A quiet summer morn is broken by crystalline splashes
Trees recess to reveal a secluded stretch of transparent water
Dare to look through the eye of a water-worn stone
And you will see something your mind may not believe
Two faeries flutter translucent wings, cup water to their breasts
As they bathe, rid themselves of night dust on slender bodies
Sun catches in the drops slithering down their skin
The shimmering jewels slip below the surface
Put down the stone now and back silently away
A glimpse is enough to create a memory of this enchanting moment

DREAM A DREAM

Let eyelids fall
And dream a dream
As easy as a feather floats

Let sun kiss you
Melt upon your skin
As easy as wind changes

Let pink lips part
Soften and invite
As easy as dew appears

Let wings relax
Sway in sweet rhythm
As easy as doves fly

Let eyelids fall
And dream a dream
As easy as a feather floats

Feathers and Braids

Home sweet home

home sweet home

The bells of home are a deeper blue
The grass is thicker and softer too
The quiet is quieter somehow
The tree is stronger from root to bough
The skies wider and more beautiful
The obligation more dutiful
The birds chirp a little more sweetly
The depth of heart fills so completely
No other place on the wide green earth
Can touch your soul as does home and hearth

ed hicks

Originally from Staten Is., NY, I've lived in New Jersey since the 60s. Went back to college at age 45 and got re-interested in art. I taught myself to paint using oils and pastels and have never looked back. My true love is portraiture and figurative work, which I've done for 20 years. I've also been teaching pastel painting for ten years. Four years ago the Faeries found me and invited me into their fantastic and magical world. Now I paint them almost exclusively.

about the paintings

All of the Faeries are painted in pastel on paper. About 90% of them are painted on sanded paper. The sizes are generally 19 1/2 x 25 1/2" (50 x 64cm) or 12 3/4 x 19 1/2" (32.5 x 50cm). Anyone interested in purchasing prints or original paintings may contact me at: edhicksartist@aol.com. My website address is: www.thefairykingdom.com

acknowledgements

I would like to dedicate this book to my wife, Cindy, for her love, support and inspiration all these years and for putting up with me disappearing into my studio at all hours of the day and night. For my kids who had faith in me. To all my lovely models, sent to me by the Faeries to portray them in this book. To Dee Stotts for finding me and keeping after me to do the book, and then finding Cameron Brown to publish it for us.

DEE STOTTS

I was born in the Philippines and grew up in sunny Florida as an Air Force brat. To this day, I still enjoy the smell of salt air and pine, the feel of warm white sand beneath my feet and sun on my face. A happily married mother of two teenage boys, I have been writing poetry since the tender age of 12. About thirteen years ago, I branched out into other genres such as children's stories and three years ago, screenplays. Writing is my heart. I can't imagine life without writing, so it came as an extraordinary pleasure to find out that, at long last, some of my work would be published. I feel very blessed.

ACKNOWLEDGEMENTS

There are so many who have touched my soul along the winding path that has brought me to this place. First and foremost, thank you, God, for bestowing me with this wondrous gift. Thank you, Tully, for it is because of you the idea of this book even came to be. Thank you, Ed Hicks, for being the most wonderful collaborator a girl could hope to work with. Thank you to my husband, Frank, for not hating me after all the long nights spent alone while I pounded away at the keyboard, and to my wonderful boys, Josh and Zac, for always believing in me and encouraging me. I always said if a publisher would believe in me half as much as you two, I would have been published long ago. Thank you, Mom and Dad for always knowing I could do it. Thank you, to all the rest of my family for the uplifting words throughout my life, especially these months I worked on this book. Thank you to Angela and Poo and Lori. Without your friendship, I would be lost. A special thanks to Ruth for all of your faith and kind words. And to all the rest of you (you know who you are) who have supported me, thank you. It is because of all of you my life is enriched.

TO THE PUBLISHER

Thank you, Cameron Brown, for this unique and wonderful opportunity.
We are delighted you took the magic of a happenstance crossing of paths and
turned it into something to be held in the hands of people across the world.
Your belief in us will not be forgotten.

Ed Hicks and Dee Stotts